Whispers From Home

Whispers From Home

Poems From Along the Journey

Michael G. O'Connor

ABUNDANT HARVEST
PUBLISHING

Editing/Formatting: Erik V. Sahakian
Cover Design/Layout: Andrew Enos

All Scripture is taken from the New King James Version of the
Bible. Copyright © 1979, 1980, 1982 by Thomas Nelson, Inc.
Used by permission. All rights reserved.

Library of Congress Control Number: 2018956509

ISBN 978-1-7327173-2-9
First Printing: December 2018

FOR INFORMATION CONTACT:

Abundant Harvest Publishing
35145 Oak Glen Rd
Yucaipa, CA 92399
www.abundantharvestpublishing.com

Printed in the United States of America

This book is dedicated to all the sojourners who travel joyfully through life, filled with the Holy Spirit, connected to the body of Christ; yet, still longing for their true home.

Contents

Preface

Much of poetry is life to me. As I live the daily flow of life, much is repeated, only in many different ways, spoken from my heart's blessing or non-blessing, only to be placed in an alignment of words which follow rhymes. At times, when reading poetry, words seem to get confusing and a bit lost in circular ideas, but they always find an ending to the beginning. This to me is life, and a part of life that I am honored and blessed to share with those who dare enter in the spinning of my mind.

In this book, many of the poems are motivated by professional experience, my own personal, spiritual struggles, and inspired moments of the mind. I think of the writer of Proverbs who penned a verse which has inspired me through the years, "Commit your works to the Lord, and your thoughts will be established" (16:3). Much of writing is not asking why or even thinking, just letting go and watching as one's mind's inspiration flows.

As you read my poems, I hope that these words are a part of life's reflection and distant darkness that can only be lit by the gentleness of the heart. In other words, my poetry is part inspired by time and used to heal as I placed pen to paper.

After many years of life, divorce, family tragedy, personal depression, and financial dismay, I have learned nothing is perfect and that we are all perfectly imperfect, living to the best of our ability, one second at a time. My travels are many in life, but the experiences of life, such as my poetry, will always bring us home.

I have been through the land of loneliness, trapped in the cave of depression and despair. Much of my journeys and spiritual struggles are sealed in the words of my directed hand, as they flow from the experiences of my mind to paper in a rhythmic rhyme called poetry. Some are dark, while others shine through the day. The darkness is where I was; the blessing of today is where I am.

My life journey has taken me to many places. Depression, loss of myself, divorce, and family death are only a part of these flowing words.

Today, I have hope in these experiences and traumas we call "life experiences" and I believe that it's only because of God's grace and love that my soul is at rest. Today, I can live with a story-filled mind, some of which I present to you, in this, the blessings of my mind.

Michael G. O'Connor

His Hand

My eyes close to the rage inside,
as I say to my heart, be still!
Does life's turmoil explode within?
Will the day's insanity cease?

As hours pass, hope breaks through;
light, once dim, now shines anew.
The rage subsides, my eyes open,
as my heart stills, beyond the broken.

Hope shines as the noonday sun
and once more God has won!
Now He gently holds me in His palm,
as I face the day, all fear is gone!

Freeing me from the burdens of life,
keeping me from this world's strife!
The rage ceases, my heart is still,
no more distraction of worldly ill.

And before me lies His hopeful plan,
as gently, peacefully, I'm led by God's hand!

Broken Vase

Cracked and battered, sitting on the floor,
pieces all around my feet.
This aged glimpse of another time,
crafted once carefully, sweetly kind.

Now cracked, shattered, pieces all around,
hopelessly broken, only pieces to be found.
Cracked, with nothing more to say,
except I must sweep what is left away.

Yet mercy serves a loving God,
as pieces of brokenness He sees.
Scars and bruises in this shattered man,
yet the beauty of hope helps me cope.

Even on my grayest day,
He lights my way, come what may.
And through life's storm, God keeps me
when days are long and life seems wrong.

God will never fail,
and by His grace, I will prevail!

Poet in the Corner

A wondering hand and written words,
scribbled in time on a page!
Things of past, enchanted dreams,
come before his eyes it seems.

Jotted down in rhythmic lines,
in simple form, gifted rhymes!
Word by word from letters appear,
before one's eyes, in beauty you hear.

Naked words from one so wise
brings a song of poetic device!
A mind, a hand, a pen, and rhyme
from within the head of a poetic mime.

Words that cling across the page,
artistic skills from life's past age.
What kind of skill makes this flow,
as nature wills this poetic glow?

Through the eyes of this one skilled hand,
flows at will, without demand.
Jotted line by line we see,
words from one, flowing free!

Knees

Gray to white,
shining down on me.
Day to night,
it brings to be!

As I look to the sky,
rain meets my eye!
I don't see,
but what I want to be!

Clearly through the gray,
I search for the warmth of day!
At last the sun comes shining through,
as on my knees I'm led back to You!

Lord, it brings me back to You!

All else seem to fade,
as in this sea I do wade.
Gray to white, day to night,
Your love comes shining through!

As my knees fall to the ground,
in Your praise, my Lord, I'm found!

Free

Lord, You give me all I need,
beyond myself and worldly greed!

Your love comes through my pain,
and, Lord, Your grace is what remains!

As You open my eyes,
in Your love I'm made wise!

Your gifts of truth and love,
You sent from above!

For it is not of me,
this I know and see.

The gifts of love and grace within me,
reign in my soul and so I'm free!

I Am

I see your tears in a crowded room,
I am there!
I feel fears from inside of you,
yes, I am near!
You cry aloud, but know you're not alone,
for my dear, your God does hear!

And in the whisper of the wind,
or silence of a sunny day,
yes, even amidst a deafening crowd,
I see! I hear! I feel!
I know, for your heart speaks aloud.

Know child that I am with you,
My love you will always see.
Through raging storms or in life's glow,
take My hand and don't let go!
For I AM right there; I already know!

Love

Each beating moment of your heart
and every breath He knows!
Every blink of your eye
and each hair on your head He's counted!

Every tear you've cried and pain you've felt,
He's held you close!
Every waking hour
and times you've said goodnight.

He knows them by days, moments of time!
He knows all your sins, sorrow, and shame.
He knows your heart! He knows your name!
He loves you! You are His joy!

He loves you
and ever His love will remain!

Broken Strings

Broken by the strings that hold my heart together,
broken and all alone.

Broken, yet in love, for brokenness you are my love.
Brokenness, I hear your footsteps go by.

Broken is my tender heart's cry, reaching out a lover's sigh.
Where must I start? Brokenhearted am I!

Broken are my love's spread wings,
consumed by love's rejections, I still cling.

Broken, unable to reach out and fly,
I turn and ask why, oh why?

Yet I watch as my heart away does fly,
as she flew away to her last goodbye!

If

If I knock will you answer?
Can you hear my heartfelt roar?
If I scream will you hear me
knocking on your heart's lonely door?

At your door will you disown me?
Oh let me die and live no more.
For in silence I die before thee,
pounding on your heart's front door.

For in silence I am before you.
Come I pray, let me in once more.

The Day

Beneath the shade tree
sits a cool running stream,
whose waters gently flow
down a hill on a sun-filled day.

I gently bow my head to pray,
peace beyond this day I see,
for each day I live by grace,
as the waters of the clear stream flow.

Grace like the shade covers me,
as life refreshing flows before my eyes,
and the gentle breeze of the day
caresses my skin.

Upon this hill nature's peace, I find,
one simple truth of God's strength entwined,
as grace I see, grace gentle and kind!
In peace I sit and leave all burdens behind.

Colors of the Rainbow

Autumn leaves fall all around!
Colors so bright
within my sight,
rained across the day in flight.

A swirling sight
in her colorful flight,
as simple leaves
dance in the breeze.

This autumn day
that God brought my way,
for me to see
His love for me.

As autumn leaves sing,
God's creation rings.
My heart dances in glee—
such a show for me!

This grand array
God brought my way,
on this blessed autumn day.

Talent Acquired

From a writer's heart.
A melody of words is
set in rhythm, set in time,
they flow together in an eccentric mime!

A talent to you!
Simply natural to do!
The pen, the paper, a wondering mind.
Together in rhythm, together combined.

A love so fond!
How does! Where does? This kind find?
Simplistically complex are words set free
from a God-given gift, wandering with glee.

This God gifting guide, in grace beauty collides.
A poet's hand writes, a rhythmical orchestral flight,
as words combine to warm the soul.

Others who read this moment do glow,
till a final plan breathes life to the show,
and all come one, together we grow.

So Many Ways

Beauty is but a moment in time,
captured by one's solitary eye,
held in one's own minute mind!

Beauty becomes what is seen
and beauty lost is beauty forgotten!
Beauty never ceases,
but is a portrait seen.

We live or we breathe true beauty each day,
as beauty comes in the form of an irreplaceable day!
Minute by minute we change;
yet, beauty is each breath we take.

The light we see, the passing stars,
or the night air free.
Beauty brings me this day
and gives me hope to light my way.

Beauty comes in so many ways!
I must thank God
for His beauty I praise!

Shalom

I will not fear nor will I wonder,
safely in Thy gentle hands.
For in Thee, my Gracious Wonder,
my Lord my King, I lay all plans!

When life's bitter trials shake me,
I know in Thee I will stand!
When this world does revile me,
I know, my God, I am but a man.

My hope is in Thy grace and power!
Yea, for peace I know, securely in Thy hands.

Calm the Storm

When comes the storm,
across the day,
my heart does rest
in a peaceful sway!

As sing my soul
in hope's array,
as on I sing
this glorious day!

What peace I see,
freeing my mind,
knowing hope
of Love so kind!

Yet sings my soul
in Thee I find,
calms the storm
within my mind.

Snow Falls

Sitting on the top of a hill,
looking down at a crowd below,
as they play beneath, under a white gray sky.

Sitting on a rock watching,
as joy across the day
brings smiles on the face of the young and old.

Then a light snow fills the air's gentle gray
and snowflakes come, touching my nose,
caressing my skin, and rolling gently down my face.

Around me the miracle of life turns to a white world!
God's presence does embrace and purity of simple grace!
Sitting, praying, as the wonder of life awakes.

Sitting on a rock, looking down on life's creation show.
Watching the day's wonder and creative joy;
praising this moment, the God I know!

Water in the Sky

Life is fishy!
Confusing to live,
fearing to die.
The day comes
and passes by.

To start again
I leave behind
who I am.
Dream to be
on the edge.

Of just me
or to be.
Closing my eyes,
opening my heart,
hoping in me.

Beyond to see
in life's circle
my head spins.
Spinning all around,
hitting the ground.

I see blind
who I am.

Looking upside down
I now drown,
looking to the sky.

I swim around
until I drown,
drowning in life.
Living profound
I now die!

Life is fishy!

Love's Sweet Release

My heart pounds within my chest,
as I stand close, but not for her to fear.
I hear my heart's rhythmic beat,
feel the gentleness of her breath so sweet,
and from a distance our eyes meet.
Together we entwine.

Love has found me,
but will I stand?
Or simply fade away
in fear to love again.
Lost in hopelessness, never to find
a love so true!

Love—a painless kind;
yet, love's sweetened song sings in my mind.
I lay entranced by the beauty, I find.
To find love!
Will love come my way?
I reach out, but in fear, I slip away!

Mary Mc

Older heart, you are my queen;
you gave, you loved, from all your being.
Without remorse, without despair,
you gave yourself without a care.

Your heartfelt love, none can compare,
and in your warmth I found solace there.
You denied yourself, ignored your harm,
and stood with beauty, grace, and charm.

I cannot but to myself be true,
for my sister, my love, I am blessed by you.

Moments

This is the beginning, not the end;
life is but a moment, desire the moment,
and live to see that there is nothing but the moment
we have!

Will there appear another moment in time to replace this?
Or will life simply go on forever, in never ceasing hours?
Alas, the truth is seen in the moment we live,
or the moment we give.

For this is the solo hour of life,
of the very thing that breathes within,
and leads us along the days, nights, and years we live.
Our life, our very existence, we live, we breathe, we are!

Lost Girl's Song

Can somebody hear me?
You know I have a voice!
In this life of madness,
please respect my simple choice.

I ask, don't you fear me?
Let me speak, please don't avoid.
I just want you to hear me;
hear my silent voice!

I long to let life love me;
I long to make it good.
Freedom that I have,
I want to live as I should!

Please, just hear me!
Respect that I have a voice.
One that will not jeer me;
please hear my hidden word.

Nights, they seem a cold, cold!
Spell of fears I within hold.
With faded dreams of a past,
I fear to see what will last.

These fears I hold deep within;

I fear a new chance or place to begin.
Yet fear I not, life's simple ways,
which keeps this heart from stray.

Till sudden hells of fearful spells
turn me from my sight!
And leave me turn to tears I know
that hold me in the night.

Oh please, just listen to my cry;
don't cast me from your sight.
Today, please hear me!
Hear my tired cry, my silent prayer's delight!

My questions why and my just I?
For I long to be the me; I am what you see.
Just me, longing to be free.
To be the who I am—yes me!

For on my own truth is sown
and nothing more.
This is what I ask for.
Hear me I ask! That's it and no more.

Before I play a final hand,
run away and fold.
Before I'm before you old,
give me a chance!

Hear me, please, and my unspoken glance.
Please let me have my chance
and dance with joy life loving dance!
Till then, I sit here in time's glance.

Time Transpires

Words inspire the words anew,
as time transpires, we see what's true!
Will the end of what we see
reflect the life of what may be?

The moment is, but we need not fear,
less fear is what we desire—we hear!
Will there be in this testy strife?
A hidden view that we see as life.

Sought

I sought a bit of love today.
I sought a touch in my own way.
A smile, a swipe, a glimpse of an eye.
From a woman's heart; from her to I!

Nothing hurtful from across my mind.
Just a woman's warm loving kind.
A soft gentle voice on a bright cheery day,
made all the difference to me on my way!

Divided Road

The windy road of pain does bear
a battered rain of one's despair.
Yet truth refrains from this affair,
for lies follow the wounded heart.

Till the road does divide,
the rainy winds subside,
and truth and pain now collide.
No more can you of yourself hide.

On the hill of one's own pride,
you tumble fast down the hillside,
into a despair in which you hide!
All along you know you lied.

Now faith alone must meet you there!
What of love? 'Tis one's own care.
For faded life you do now wear,
as to yourself, you do now share.

What of life?
Beyond one's strife!
As faded years now cut as a knife
and past decay, today hurtful wrong.

Now you cling to what makes strong!

In this life's vaporously short, short song,
'tis a stanza or a simple dong,
which leads to truth in one's own life long.

Minute by Minute

Miraculously, minute by minute
the gift of time we share,
breathes marvel and gives us life!
The beating heart beats in time.

Amazing is this gift called life!
Yet, limited is this gift called life.
As day by day this mystery takes hold
and before we see we are now old.

Before the heart does cease!
Before our last breath sighs!
And to this life we say goodbye
as we live in the gift each today.

In hope that tomorrow is long,
in hope that life will never sleep;
yet, of a truth today we must keep!
Time is a gift from the Giver of all.

The Giver's love is true,
who hears each heartfelt call.
Who knows the hour of our days
and loves us all in our ways!

Our lungs with air do fill,

though seek we will,
His love fulfills.
Beyond a ceasing heart's will.

So as an eternal song,
His love does live on.
An eternal long
life full song!

Content

Palm trees dance in the warm summer air
as clouds of cotton hang with such care.
Amidst the blueness of the sky,
a bright day's majesty before my eyes.

Life lives and breathes such grace;
I thank my God for this time, this place!
Moments I have this very hour,
peacefully me, this day does shower.

Years of my life all in one place
as I sit content in time's space!
Palm trees dance on this created day
as I thank my God for His awesome display.

What Do I Do?

What do I do
when what I do I do?

When I do what I done?
When what I done I did?
When done I did what?

What do I do with what I done
when I did what I did?

What do I do?
Yet what is done is done.

Hidden Me

Events in my life lead me to despair's feeling
of hopelessness.
The thoughts and beliefs of who (what) controls me inside
leads me back to the hidden me, from whom I hide.

Till the truth of who I truly am leads me to see
and open my eyes.
I see the man I really am, beyond the chains of life's pains,
unshackled by the hands of honesty,
truth is released and remains!

I am perfectly broken in life's lesson learned
and find consistent truth's daily churn.
Perfectly placed in one's daily fire,
I find of truth my own desire.

Days of the past I leave behind;
memories now a part of my mind.
As age now holds me in her hand,
wrinkled now from my once youthful plans.

Running once with youthful legs,
I ran through life with a bit more aged pegs.
Helping me along my daily way,
leading me on to meet today!

Regret will I not today's milieu
as tomorrow, tomorrow I live a true!
For hopeless despair once held my mind,
till I learned peace of the aged kind.

So will I regret the days I live
or hold on tight to lessons life gives?
Aged hands I do now hold,
but thank the Lord 'tis His perfect mold!

Mystic Blue Eyes

A pair of jeans and mystic blue eyes
catch my attention.
My, oh my!

A glowing woman's beauty;
I'm captured in her spell!
Entranced by her beauty,
in her sensuousness I dwell.

Her eyes hold me lost in space,
without a concept of self or place!
Her smile reaches my inner soul
and leaves me lost in a deep, dark hole.

Feeling good about the mess I'm in—
mystic blue eyes and jeans so smooth.
You look so good, so beautiful; a sheer delight
as you breathe today, here before my sight.

Through the Trees

Through the trees I see the other side of where I am.
On the other side I see what lies before my eyes.
There I see a distant look at what is!
A present sight I see till I see no more.

Till what lies before me dies.
Till in death I see no more!
As I close my eyes and never more to open,
in this day in this time!

Through the trees I see the other side.
In death I will see beyond the trees of eternity,
to what lies in front of me, I will see!
I will know that death's final side leaves me to see.

Beyond the day, to the eternal show of life.
Beyond this day! Beyond this hour!
Beyond the world that I now see!
Beyond 'tis now I truly see…

Long Lost Friend

Strangely simple, confusingly complex, is the mind of man.
The way of man in love is strange,
as his heart patters along.
Yet when love dies and anger fills love's void,
how does one heal in time's hurtful long?

For time does not remove the scars of a broken heart;
yet in time love does find her way home.
Viciously deceptive is bitterness to one's heart;
destroying one's feeling of love's return.
Tearing one's soul right from a heart,
bitterness destroys any hope of love's desire.

To love again 'tis the heart's true desire,
for hope 'tis found beyond the past's pain.
Yet love can be wisely cautious a second time around,
as the cold wind of rejection warns a willing heart!

Not to question love's truth second sound.
Love remains a long lost friend,
rediscovered when truth evades past pain.
Time's healing hand brings love to love's joy long lost!

Differently the same in time's healing wane,
the fire of love's friendship will be rekindled again!
Though some choose a solo life,

love's healing truth within remains.
As we learn life is not what we see or do;
love is the heart's true.

As scars of life subside you are never more alone,
for the truth of love's desire is from within.
To you, this is where love does begin.
From within without love is rising
and once again seen!

Land of the Free

Sitting on the edge of the world as I know it,
looking west to the ocean's flow.
The Atlantic behind, the Pacific ahead,
my back turned to the home I love.

Focused on the seas of beyond,
how life has changed from my days as a youth.
The complexity of this world I know as life;
the land of the free has lost her way.

As free is now at a cost
of other's dreams, these now lost.
Domestically we have lost our way,
forgetting our own truth, godlessly we now stray.

Our greedy attire seeks just one more to acquire.
A political feast of fattening spoils;
campaign promises and greedy toils.
Too big to fail! So sacrifice too less!
We scramble the truth into a sickening mess.

Sitting, looking out over the ocean,
my eyes filled with tears.
A heavy heart, as I see the face of America dying!

Question

I'm not the answer, I'm the question.
Unless the question is the answer.

Then I know that I know that life is a puzzle!

A breathing sequence of unknown,
unproven, unsure questions placed before our day.

If you question the answer,
then the answer is always a question!

We are always asking truth is always an unknown.
We are always learning! Life is always progressing!

Till life's questions cease and breath sees her end.

Life is no more, we question no more.
No more no less, as all answers move to life's eternal place.

I'm not the answer this is true,
but truly is the question life's true!

On the Hill

Sitting on the top of the hill,
rolling life over in my mind.
Looking for solutions to my broken heart,
sitting on the hill hoping to unwind!

On my way to fifty years old,
on my own from love I've known.
Love gone cold as life grows old.
Will I know?

Searching for warmth before I'm old!

Take it All

Who can save me from this day?
For I fear the night to fall!
Who can deliver me from my way?
For I hear the beacon call!

Oh light, please shine upon my way;
direct me or I fall.
Oh sight, fail not my vision today;
hear, I pray, my call.

For in this hour I am dismayed;
help me to stand tall.
Before I scour and run away,
God help me! Please take it all.

A Depressed Man's Song

I don't long to give up on life,
but to give up on what steals my life.
What drags me into my cave's demise
of the coldness and sadness, a dark dreary mire?
Self-pity's negative attire!

What can I do when I can't see past me?
Misery keeps me in a hard shell
of sadness's bitter demise.
I sit, lost behind my self-lies.

Consumed all around, I scream so loud!
In a voiceless crowd I scream, but no one hears.
Life around me, emotionally
flawed and broken, I hide in shame.
Of who and what, what and who?

Depression only answers me with pain;
the fears of what and who in life remains!
So I hide in fear of another day,
hoping tomorrow's hope may be found.

I must live to see the me that could be,
so I reach for hope's compassion
with a desire to be free.
Beyond this hopeless, self-pitying me!

[57]

Stories

Stories from a storybook chime,
across the children's hearts by a mime.
Stories of past, present, and future in time;
words, some true, others simply a rhyme.

Stories of both near and far,
come to meet them where they are.
The mind of a child, a well sealed jar,
seals them in and sets them on par.

For life to a child is each day anew
and words that they hear are all true.
So come what may, much or few,
to a child a story is to their life a clue.

Divorce

Fast divorce, read the sign in place.
Slow for love it took the place.
No time for love's beauty and grace.
Just forget true love, get out of my space.

Shallow is this modern time,
for it knows not love's longing pine.
When things don't work we draw the line
and simply dispose of what is mine.

Trust is a word quickly thrown away,
only to treat love as a delay.
Lost in time is the simple way,
when we look to each other, sit down and pray.

Come, oh heartfelt love, be true.
Come, my love, bring me back to you.
Read the sign that is not blue
and replace it with love, for love's ever true.

Brother

To my brother, my friend, my accomplice,
and my mother's son.
My heart rings with songs of joy
amidst the sadness within your voice.

For you have been a pillar of faith,
an example to me along this life's road.
While time moves on to life's long send,
we both will walk till each breath's end.

Side by side and hand in hand, you're my brother,
my sibling, and my friend.
Together we've seen God's mercy and glean;
in His hands we place all we have and what we've been.

His eyes stare to this world's lonely skies
and know that our song is the hope of beyond.
As our Lord gladly waits at His precious gates
to welcome us home and no more be alone.

As brothers, we two will be restored anew,
as by God's healing hand we enter His plan.
To my brother, my friend, in this world we have an end,
but together, we two, eternally renew.
Fellowship up above, forever in His love!

The Winding Road

The day was warm, as a smell of spring's excitement,
colors, and grace illuminated the day; I slowly inhaled all
God's beauty and stood in His presence, so profound.

I partook of the path before me.
This fine April Irish morning the birds sang melodiously of
life as the day was born; a symphonic beauty chimed,
creation from the Master's hands, blessing this early morn.
Red, blue, yellow, green—every color danced in an
unrehearsed waltz of perfection.

All this selection came before me, God's creation so
profound, as I strolled, touching my feet on this wonderful
ground, unrehearsed nature did sing, a perfect ensemble of
praise to the King.

How great a Creator, how could anyone doubt?
All this only could be created by a Masterful God.
Oh wondrous creation this morning,
a day of His spectacular presence.

I strolled for miles all through the day,
up the hills and through the valleys far, far away,
beyond the pastures of green-blue skies, mossy brown
walls of stone, and mountains high.
Upon the hills I strolled without a care, just He and I,

as the noon sun rose above the mountains high.

I strolled with my Savior, I had not an ill nor a care.
As the sun rose high, life glistened and gleaned.
Sheep, cows, and horses were all grazing without a care;
great was the feast of God's wondrous beasts.
The evening drew nigh and I strolled forth in the shire;
I dare not stop for I had no desire.

Up the hill I continued away, then finally stopping for a
little while on the way, the sun shined and I took time to
pray, as the breeze caressed my face once more
near fields of hay.

I listened and heard tiny ants all around, scurrying busily at
much that they found, and bees busy buzzing around in
time, gathering in their feast-filled chime.

I met with God upon the way; we spoke in tune as I
stopped and prayed.
Thankfully, I was blessed in this place and time;
thanks to God who is so kind.
We met as we stopped along the way;
I continued and I walk with God to this day!

The Old Mantle Clock

The old mantle clock brings forth a story-filled sound;
tick-tock, tick-tock on its never ending round.
It moves into time with a melodious sound;
aged hands conduct reach to direct the pound.

With gentleness and care, watch time bring us there,
and reaches out to rewind without despair.
Stepping back and in a confident stare,
watches ticks move in and tocks bring us there.

Hands greeted in this symphonic sigh,
now youthfully greet its next beaconing cry.
Tick moves on in and tock passes by;
Tick-tock, tick-tock, young to old, goodbye!

Easterly Wind

The wind blew across the dusty desert floor;
easterly strong and around through my door.
I stood and gazed at the power and more;
yet never once feared the wind's roar.

I am a man, I am nothing more;
a man whose wings long to soar.
Yet in the wind-filled desert floor,
the wind does wield and come to roar.

In a whisper comes a sound;
a whoosh of wind can be found.
Peaceful calm below the mound,
as the wind subsides to peace around.

Calmness comes upon the ground,
as dust settles in a downward pound.
No more through my door a gusty bound,
for no more the day the wind does hound.

Shattered

My world was shattered this very day;
my heart sunk deep within.
Battered and torn this very day;
my heart was torn apart.

My life became a deep, deep well;
my heart was lost within.
My love now coldly sways from me;
my heart did with her depart.

Where Does Love Go?

Where does love go when the feeling is gone?
Does love simply dissolve as many say?
Or do those who loved simply lose sight?

What once was so strong does not dissipate.
Unless the wandering heart meets her fate.
Yet wander as she may there is no debate.

For new love now fulfills none the more.
Till once again the heart wanders for.
As restless love knows no greater than.

The first and true; where it all began.
So I will ask once again!
Is love's feeling where all should end?

Or does feeling truly know love's end?

Tears in the Glen

Across the glen and mountains glow,
my love awaits for this I know.
My heart afire a heaven's flow,
up the hills and down so low.
Across the heathers I go,
ah, to my love, my love so.
To see, to feel you, oh!

My heart does pound
for thee profound.
I move, yet not a sound,
to thee my love.
To thee my love astound.
I came, I looked all around
for thee, my love not found.

So here I sit in deep despair,
as I turn and look if you are there.
Alas you're gone, I know not where,
as I reach forth to stroke your precious hair
and caress your skin, oh so fair.
I am but a man whose heart must bear
in this life, love's crushing air!

Mudder

Mother, why do you try so hard
to win a love that did not cease?
Ah Mother, know in peace
a wayward son I may sometimes be.

My heart will always be here with thee,
even among the storms of life.
In the midst of worldly strife,
Mother, you are and will always be.

The one in whom I am free,
through this life I will look in glee.
To you my Mother, in you I see
what I've become and I want to be!

Wrinkles

I look in the mirror and see the hands of time
whisper across the years of rhythm and rhyme.
Eyes of green on an aged face.

'Tis my own reflection I see
staring back, dreaming of "used to be."
I am in all ways still me.

Except for my youthful glee,
my eyes see within me.
Forever to myself I will always be!

Cracked

What can I be beyond a broken heart?
As I look at the brokenness and parts,
can I seek? Can I restore?

What can mend the pieces left inside
or will I be lost in a loveless array?
I am powerless over this emotional me!

Of myself, I cannot be free.
Without God, all of my will to be
can leave me with nothing more than me!

Heather Morn

Gray stone and heather—
this the misty Irish morning.
'Tis another day of traditional rain,
across the mystic Irish plain.

Centuries meet across the day
as Irish fields of green do sway.
For this, a solitary moment in time,
awakens my heartfelt Celtic rhyme.

Gray stone and heather, a jubilant sight—
my past meets present in traditional flight.
For what was is now and will forever be,
my traditional heart as it longs to be free!

Forever with God

To live we know no less than death,
if hope is in our God!
In death we live far beyond,
for now hope is our God's.

One day in our eternal home,
no more to end or roam.
For in Thy great eternal light,
no more to slip or lose Thy sight.

Forever with God, my power and might,
no more to sin for we win the fight.
Eternal hope, by day and by night,
forever we sing in our eternal flight.

Eternal Hope

When all our days come to an end
and all die loved ones and friends.
As hearts grow old as time does not lend,
eternal hope is all we do send.

For dreams come and pass us by,
and beauty turns to an age old sigh.
From birth to death man does cry,
for hope only comes as redemption draws nigh!

In man's loneliness God's fulfillment begins,
as eternity reaches out and man enters in.
No more fear, no more death, no more sin,
as victory breaks forth, now we do win!

Slipping

I slip so easily from the path I'm on;
I fall in a deep dark hole.
I slip like a rock as emotions con;
I call as I search my soul.

I slip down and further on;
God reaches out as I downward roll.
To lift me up, no more to con,
and saves my slipping soul.

The Town I Know

A smoke-filled shroud,
amidst brick homes proud—
a sooty chill fills the air.

Smoke-filled chimney stacks,
as chattering smiles, "What's the craic?"
and warm faces pass me by.

In this ancient town, life all around,
as children meet and families greet.
There is her heart! This town so sweet!

Glowing strong in her day-to-day song,
of love's lived fright and years of flight.
Her ancient story of tears and glory!
Yes, 'tis the town I know!

On mothers' faces of years worn but true,
and fathers' elations of boyhood dreams anew,
live strong in their children's songs,
as generations pass through.

Wind felt change of tomorrow arrange,
blow on through, yet her traditions remain.
This is the town; the town I know!

Where love and peace I've found;

yes, even beauty in her sooty surround!
Where my heart became and my heart is found!

In this old town!
For here, me I see,
and for here I'm found.

Another Scratch Found

How years go by on the LP of life.
A few scratches, a bit outdated, but they still roll along.
As the record plays one's lifelong song,
memories of past times and years grow strong.
A bit dusty and dirty, but still they play on!

A classic of one's time's rhythm and rhyme.
Untouched but for a scratch or two through a lifetime.
A classic, an oldie, yet still it is mine,
plays on her beauty in the corner of my mind.
For life's LP is forever so gentle, so kind!

'Tis

Love can be profound;
life can bring dumfound!
The desires of the heart;
our heart's internal fires.

Love seeks a way;
life's desire seeks love's sway.
Fear can steal a soul away;
yet a soul is not to fear!

Along this, life's winding road,
love's lost tears bring a heavy load.
For love's loss can isolate in her shame,
and love's lost time is what remains.

Yet the heart desires what love acquires,
unless life's isolation remains.
But a memory of a love, now gone,
hides the hope of how to move on.

Living in truth, to yourself be kind,
and love will to you find.
Life will live beyond the shame—
accept that life does remain!

For in love's remains, there the heart sounds.

The Words of a Heartfelt Man

Man's heaviness stems from emptiness within—
his lack of direction, his selfishness, his sin.
Living an empty self-seeking desire,
he rages within in a defeating fire.

Blindness becomes his sight full acquire,
as he remains stuck in a hapless mire.
Stumbling through life, desiring a way home,
he is bound to wander; he is bound to roam.

Till the truth comes and God's light is seen!
Does one see the truth of what life does mean?
Light comes to a darkened night;
He sees in wrong, God made it right.

Truth found awakens, restores, renews, and revives.
The deadness of his soul now becomes alive!
As hope, desire, and love lead on,
beyond an empty life there lives a new song.

Heaviness no longer reigns; hope is the light he sees!
Finding safety one becomes free;
free to be and safe in He.
Free to be forever free!

Quiet Storm

I whisper to the one I love;
I whisper her name.
I whisper, yet nothing do I hear.
What of this dreadful pain?

I whisper, but alas inside I scream!
I smile through the torrential shame—
a love lost, a heart broken.
Tears flow in the heart of this man.

Yet live I must; yet live I will again!
Beyond pain a heart that knew love
and desires to love; desires to be free to love.
I whisper to the one I love.

Yes, I whisper her name.

Drunken Hour

Dazed and staggering through the day's burning light,
the smell of the sinking sun falling from sight,
creating torturously a glare of tomorrow's morn!
Just another, my man! One more 'twill help me stand.
Or stagger through the drowning day's demand!

Ah! Just a dram; a pint, a hit I ask!
One for the road! Hit me once, promise 'tis the last!
Dazed and staggering, forgetting there's an end,
as wasted hours spent with one's intoxicating friend.

Life passing in a dull drunken sight,
ignoring the foolishness of one's drunken blight.
Losing glimpse of life, drunker by the hour,
till all around life turns quickly sour.

Till death of the senses clears all thoughts that be;
one turns so blind one no longer can see.
Just another, before I go dry!
Alas, this is the drunkard's goodbye!
In this an alcoholic's world denies!

Refuse to Hate

Hate will not bear my name; I will love my fellow man.
I will live love and not share hateful pain.
In life I may see injustice, hurting, and pain.
Yet today I choose to let love remain!

Not because I am perfect, nor undo shame,
but I stand in peace to live life that remains.
I stand to live love, to love all by Your name!
I choose to see the good in my fellow man.

I will not fear to live this day
and will respect all in life's plan.
I refuse to hate or debate the viciousness of man,
for I live this life in peace where I stand.

The hateful heart of disunity,
the calloused heart of man's hateful desire,
which only leads to useless acquire
as death comes.

Done!

Another! Just one!
Promise, then I'll be done.
Before the morning rises to another sun,
I need a drink to make me think about none.

Ah, just one! One to be done!
To slow my aching head, just one.
Through empty eyes I live my lies and within tears flow,
but 'tis me that truly does know.
Unless I have one more to go!

As the sun rises, I hide behind disguises
of who I see in me—I hide!
Ah, just one! So no one can see,
before the shadow of me that lives in sour
comes to life in my drink-less hour.

Alas, not another sober moment in time;
I pray let me pass it drunkenly blind.
For I need a sip to please my mind,
as life slips away and I forget to find.

Hobo Jack

Hobo Jack is always on time,
with his scented smell of whisky and wine.
A beat up sack from a war he knew,
and boots he marched in, once proud and true!

An old pair of torn jeans, worn Levis,
and a bottle of booze to wear a disguise!
He walks and talks along his way;
is he crazy or is this simply a display?

See, Jack came back from a war he knew,
and became a prisoner from all he held true.
Hostage to the world's word, "succeed";
losing the truth in this world's selfish greed.

Now a dime, a nickel, a penny or two,
Jack edges his way to all he holds true.
A bottle of whiskey or wine, a few,
leads him to sing a chord for you.

Yet as he passes you might see him cry,
as sobering thoughts of his pass by.
Taking a hard swig from the bottle is his reply;
toxically polluted his feelings subside.

Insulated by the isolation he chooses,

he lives his life numb from emotional bruises.
Intoxicated with denial he drinks till he falls,
fearing life's truths and her sobering calls.

Yes, Hobo Jack is always on time,
within his own alcoholic mind.
As he sees and lives life drunkenly blind,
one more drink is what weighs on his mind.

He drinks away truths painful shiver
and burns away life from his hurtful quiver.

Sitting

On my bed, thoughts circling my mind,
wishing to stop, wishing to unwind.
Around and around, and around I go!
This mind! This never ending creation flow.

What can be of this restless world?
For all around this circus clown
plays with words and disarrays,
of imagination within me.

I long to create, yet hope to be free!
Words come; words and circles I see,
as poetic space encircles me.
I write and write, around and around,
and somehow rhythm within is found.

Is this a space of creation I see?
Or a craze that lives inside of me?
Yet stop not I will, nor can I not free,
the craziness of life some call poetry.

Breathe!

Everyday life begins or ends.
This gift celebrated may seem long,
but to those who lived, short is her song!

As youthfulness strives to obtain,
there are many who strive to remain,
while others obtained to live life in vain.

This life's venture some see to deny,
as childhood and youth passes them by.
Truth blurred closes their eyes to what remains
and while living to self, they work to remain.

Living to love is foreign and unknown,
spending it all in the fearing zone.
To oneself, fearing, living alone;
hurtful in life, they live the unknown!

Fearing loneliness, they desire to connect,
but connection's pain and hurtful shame
causes one to run; yet, in running they seek to find
who or what truly lies inside.

Yet in finding the pain, they seek to hide,
and in hiding fear truth, fear time, fear youth!
Seeking peace in life is out of control,

as clinging to what one does not know.

Then a blink of the eye before one nods their head
and life goes from birth to a tombstone—dead!
Never living many live, fearing to try
to live today's beauty before time passes by.

Everyday life begins and every life dies.
Know you do not need to be victim to her hateful lies.
Live this very moment for it never will remain
and breathe the wondrous miracle that runs in your veins!

Passing

Through distance and years, I watch time pass by.
How can I be so blind to the love by my side?
I hear the breath of time and face my fearful love;
through my shyness I feared to let love free.

Only now to see beauty that is there!
Through distant fears I lived in shame,
silently I loved as fear remained.
Stepping out to fall back, I smile to a frown.

Live to love, yet still I restrain alone,
yet love is all around.
As I watch years pass me by,
awkwardly fulfilled, I live, just I!

Reaching out to love, longing to love;
how can I be blind?
I ask as I hear the breath of time,
shyly recoiled by the childish me.

I see the beauty around; I call out her name.
Silence fills my lungs; I scream, yet no one hears,
but my fears through the years of love lost.
Without a sound, I live in love's profound.

Beating Heart

Hello, to a friendly heart.
I thank God you beat;
I hear you sweet.
Hello, my friendly heart!

Hello, my warm glow.
I watch you grow
within life's flow.
Hello, my warm heart!

Hello, my precious smile.
I see such glee
upon lips of memory.
Hello, my precious smile!

Oh, beating heart and warming glow,
your precious smile about me grows.
For I hear your heart's sweat plea!

I feel the warmth of your loving glow
and tender lips that smile an embrace,
to this beating heart's holy space.

Hello, my beating heart!

Fixedly Broken

Bright is the night of man's empty soul,
as shines the mind's desire to be whole.
As years of tears and desperate control
break, longing to fill the loss within the soul.

Eyes turned to the skies longing to know,
truly truth and where must I go?
Dimly man sits in life's empty hole,
till the mind entwines God's warming glow.

One sees through years of tears, fears do control,
and eyes of lies only confuse what one does know.
To find the place and space to begin by grace,
reaching out in honesty you shout!

Grace is the space beyond pain, beyond sin, beyond shame;
tears of the years God knew by name.
He hears the fears, knows the shame,
and heals the wounds beyond the pain.

Each heartfelt prayer, each moment of despair—
He was there!
There is where He held you close;
yes, in the time you needed Him most!

God give you hope beyond your cope;

He relieves the storm, calms the day,
and keeps you strong in life's disarray.
Within life vies, He brings calm peaceful skies.
For within the veil we prevail
and an empty soul now lives whole!

Rhythm and Rhyme

Mystic eyes amidst a warm smile,
there you are in my mind.
Though separated by miles and time,
I hear a gentle whisper of your voice.

In completeness beauty sings,
a perfect rhythm and rhyme.
This craziness of words now come to flow;
not words to fear what you hear,
but in craziness to warm the heart.

A place to start and let you know,
the amazing part of the you I know!

Thanksgiving

Momentous.
Brightness of a winter day.
Chilly air's momentous sway.
A Thanksgiving eve's bustling crowd.
Excitement fills the day in a shroud.
A festive near is here, as friends and families
draw now near, the stores jingle as crowds prepare
for the presence of remembrance and thankfulness.
For all that God allows and hearts of gratefulness
bring chimes of joy at this day's Thanksgiving.
To each and all in this time we are living.

Pretty Girl

This day brings to mind
years one has left behind
and through their tears
life's shattered jeers,
which may once seem unkind.

Know the smile upon your face
as you breathe life's glory and grace,
and around you truth comes to this race
for beauty bears your name!
Smile by smile today hope is enflamed.

Pretty girl, know that you'll find
that the years are more than kind,
though fears of the years
now left behind
travel much upon your mind.
Pretty girl, life is kind.

Tears now have dried
and words of youth tell the truth—so kind!
Pretty girl, I see in you one so genuinely true
as life's constant burning flame
conquers years of toil and shame.

Pretty girl, know your beauty does not fade

for you're beautifully and wondrously made,
and God holds you—even knows you by name!
Pretty girl, know that I am
a simple messenger,
a caring friend!

Don't fear the dance; live life's prance.
In hopeful of dreams, it's God who gleams
the precious most.

September

The first cold rain.
Michael Lynch's shop, a gold red presence
radiates across the way,
as a chilly rain falls all around!

Eoin's Pub a glimpse away;
I feel the chill of the day.
Mid-September ushers in a chilly stray;
cars pass by and lightly spray.

This rainy, chilly day.
Summer's left, can't stand this cold;
my bones are stiff this side of old.
I lift my eyes to the rain.

Breath within the moistening air,
so freshly clear this chilly air.
Some scamper by, hiding from the rain,
others plod on with umbrellas raised.

A guard struts by in his winter coat,
his peaked hat pulled down
and collar covering his throat.
The shuffle of the busy town.

Move quickly so it won't get drowned!

[97]

The ruffle and shuffle down Clanbrassil Street,
amidst the spraying of the street and traffic's
rhythmic beat, 'tis another autumn on her way.

Coldly she comes, boldly for none,
as the way turns the day yearns.
The summer's beat turns to autumn's feet,
on this cold Dundalk morn.

Music of the Day

Ta-ta-rat-tat-tat!
Or something that goes just like that.
Brum-brum-brum!
Here it comes.

A star-shined night,
one of delight.
The music of the day fills the air
as once a sun-filled day.

No concerns for the gray
as night leads to a calming morning.
This from an evening of delight;
lives come my way and joyful music does play!

Tut-de-tut, bam-de-bam!
We all come together in life's lovely plan.
Night to morning, delight blows her horn,
and smiles and laughs at a joke or two.

Life's delightful dance;
don't lose out for it's but a glance.

Wrinkled Hands

Hands wither in a lifelong parade,
a day, a year, a minute to hours.
Passing truths of memories cower,
words said now linger in time.

Memories—some painful, some kind—
hold me; I am in my mind.
Wrinkled hands now slow in time,
as all we become a rhythm and rhyme.

Hope holds us to what is true,
to the heart that be and who I see.
At times I close my eyes to the word "life,"
within my own with closed eyes I see.

Contently, I must learn to accept my me
and look to God who makes me free.
Death is but a simple end,
no more to live to life defend.

Sing we all must a final song
and reach to God's eternal strong.

Amends

Fear the morn, alas her ayre!
Amidst the life-felt tares,
awake I do in hope and care.
Words amidst one's own aware.

Dashed to a heart of a friend's fire,
at times dragged through the worldly mire.
Spoken as a sword's piecing pain,
only fear of life does remain.

Fear not love in one's stricken heart!
For my heart, once broken, heals with no shame.
Ah! Of truth hurt, loss does remain;
yet a hurtful past tends to inspire.

When controlling the heat consumes my shallow shell,
rekindling the truth of love truth found.
For it is not what I do with a broken life,
but what I do with the brokenness in my life.

Life is full of great divides and in pain lives collide,
but what of who I am?
This is the truth that will lead me far!

Here

I'm sitting here loving, loving you in my life!
I feel your heart's beating motion,
the gentleness of your lips on mine,
the warmth of your body's life.

I feel you, I see you, I love that you are mine!
Lady of beauty, sweet love I find,
from a gentleness so kind,
you bring love so wonderfully fine.

As I hold you close, my world stands still!
I breathe with you; it's you I inhale.
Here I am, love in my life.
Here, my love!

Here I am, here for love's life!

Taking Hold

Hidden behind the eyes of a man,
there lives love's strange desires,
of what he holds as really true.

A woman reaches deep into his soul,
takes hold of his heart,
and flows like blood through his veins.

Raptures the life he once knew;
brings him love,
makes him love.

Hidden behind the eyes of a man,
love's desires are so strange,
only a woman knows the plan!

Self-Protective Song

Tears drip down my face!
Why are you not here with me?
Dry I must my tearful revile,
as I sit and listen for a while.

Hearing my own internal me,
as I say to myself, what will be will be!
Tears they cease, but linger on,
as my heart beats the "I've lost you" song.

Time moves on to whispers, then subsides,
as missing you, deep within, I now hide.
Forgetting and moving on, I lie to myself once more,
as I mourn the loss in a self-protecting song!

Roller Coaster

Life is full of ups and downs.
Fear not life! Take a look around
to see life's wonders profound.
Fear not the dance life brings,
but follow each step, each beat in time.

Accept God's love-filled pleasures
and hold on tight to His many treasures.
Let Him shelter you within His arms
and guide you close, free from harm.
Life is full of hurtful pains;
yet by His grace, He heals our shames!

Ups will go down and downs just the same;
yet hope in God will always remain.
He will be a guiding light,
as we stumble blindly without sight.

God will bring a peaceful flow
and comfort us when we do not know.
Up and down this life we lead,
but in His love we are freed.

Where Do Wars Come From?

Where do wars come from?
Words, whims, and angry hearts;
man's disagreements and selfish greedy desires.
Hatred of our fellow creation—ourselves!
Striving for control, for power,
we destroy what is not truly ours.

In the viciousness of our limited minds,
we justify the mayhem and atrocity of our inexplicable lies!
Driven on by hate, we destroy God's creation;
a divided world beyond our own disbelief.
War takes no enemies, killing all it leaves behind,
as we relive death in war's chasm of despair.
Living yet dying, healing yet wounded;
scarred within our hatred for our fellow man,
as man's hatred now becomes years maimed in time.

So what of war?
What of man's disagreements?
Selfish is our heart's desire;
without the hope only of God
we kill, we destroy, and we live to disagree.
War is not without the truth we see—
man and his own selfish, angry, and deceitful heart!

Broken Man

The ayre of Jackson Browne rings in my ears,
drowning out the lost heart's sorrowful pain.
So a glass of wine brings a mellow moment,
becoming time's friend,
and lightens the load of this wounded heart's pain!
Not a permanent fix, just a relaxing moment in time.

I am the product of my generation's stain
for I am fifty-two and on my own!
A bit lost, a bit found in an unsure world of the profound.
An unforgiving time, where greed is the only love found;
where the common man is held down
by the desire to be free.
Deceived by corporate greed to hold down
and leave only to need.

Yet here I live in a product of the life I now have—
tipsy, lonely, but still alive to face the day's new light.
Caught in the present hour's hope and life's remain.
"Sorrows that keep me afloat in the hours life offers;
fountains of sorrow, fountains of life!
You know that hollow sound of your own steps in flight?
You've had to hide sometimes, but now you're all right!"

When we see through life's illusions there is the sight.
It's an amazing feeling when we see beyond

what hides behind deception.

Not that life is a deception! No, not at all!
Rather, life hides behind what we fear,
what we see beyond our fear to see, or fear to be.
Do I fear? Or simply do I hide my fears
and see life beyond the life I know, beyond the life to be?

Now Jackson sings on in my heart, in my pain,
"I hold words of sorrow's refrain!
Ah, the life of the pretender—do it again! Amen!"

Meanwhile, I order another glass of wine
and hope that somehow life's pain will refrain.
I am but a broken man in a full piece of existence,
striving to prove myself ok.
Till one day I break free of this stifling life
and move on to the other side.

I hope that somehow I will be found
and God will have mercy on this wandering soul.
That God will see the pain of this life I lived
and show me mercy's open door.
"Running on empty! Running blind!"

So now what of life? I don't know!
All I know is life goes fast; life leaves time behind.
I sit and wonder—what truly I wish to find!

Love Through the Day

I sit looking out on the street—
you are there!
I see people busy across the day—
you are on my mind!

I feel the gentle wind caress my face—
your eyes bring me to smile!
I hear a love song through the day—
your voice steals my heart away!

I walk this city's streets alone,
holding you close in my heart.
I continue through the day;
I dream of us walking side by side.

Loving you from end to start,
my love through the day, you fill my heart!

I Wish

There are things I wish I'd said.

I wish I'd smiled just right.
I wish I'd held a woman real tight.

I wish I'd kissed the lips I longed to.
I wish I'd spoken my mind more true.

I wish I'd looked more into beautiful eyes.
I wish I'd held strong instead of goodbyes.

I wish I had, but alas I did not.
I wish that I had not forgot!

My Open Door

The pureness, the beauty!
Your eyes and smile!
You captured my heart.
Nothing do I revile!

Now distant, different lives we lead.
Yet in this heart are words not freed!
So will you now please enter in?
For I wish to tell you, 'tis no sin.

To open once more
my heart's hidden door.
Open, come see!
To you it's all free!

Take what you want;
it's my heart's gift to you.
Take a look and see
what you really mean to me!

Showers of Blessings

Oh, to roam in life
across the shadow's day
through valleys long.

Across dales, as rain hails,
upon the longing soul
comes hope's whispering flow.

Amidst the rays of sun-filled days
the hands of time meet the hands of love,
as roam I may.

Shadows make way to the light
of God's loving glow,
to hope only in truth to know.

As high mountains bow,
and streams of life flow,
dales of rain hail.

Showers of blessings
upon those who come His way,
stand in peace this blessed day!

No Doubt

Love is a strange and mighty thing!
Love is! Love is!

We'd walk a mile, or a hundred, or two,
to feel the pain and yet still remain.

Funny how the mind does dwell
when set array in lustful play!

Ah, love is but a word we sing,
or throw about as a meaningless shout!

Yes, love is a strange and mighty thing!
No doubt! No doubt!

Love's Prayer

It's one a.m., just past a Friday night,
and sleeping right now just doesn't seem right.
My wheels are turning and I can't sleep tonight,
thinking of you and are you all right?

I pray to God above to cover you in His love
and hold you tight tonight!
As I close my eyes I see your face—
are you asleep?

I hope it's ok to say I love you!
I want to hold you close tonight,
if that's all right?
I ask the Savior to bless your sleep's sweet flight.

I bow my knees and say in a simple way,
"God, protect her; please keep her safe tonight
and just, Lord, hold her close tonight.
I just really give You her this night."

Lord, I know she's safe in Your sight!
Yes, God, I love You and I know it's all right!

Gentle

I am a whisper of the wind;
I am a ruffle in the leaves!
I am a heart that feels love's pain;
I am what of love does remain.

I am love's losing game;
I am a heart of lonely shame.
I am the smoldering of love's flame;
I am this man, I have a name!

For I am just a simple man;
I am a man without a plan.
I am the ruffle of the leaves;
I am the whisper of the wind!

I am from a heart of pain;
I am all that does remain!
I am as a ruffle of the leaves;
I am just what I believe.

Hope—this is what remains—
love's freedom still sustains!
And beyond the pain and hurtful shame,
I know, love's beauty does remain!

Beauty

We long to see beauty,
to touch beauty's face.
We look around for beauty,
yet beauty lives from within.

Beauty comes in the desire to live;
beauty comes in the desire to give!
Beauty is beyond what a body lives;
within our hearts and hopes she lives!

Beyond this beauty asks not much,
but that we accept embrace, not clutch!
Beauty is a calming fan,
which warms the heart of every man.

Whispers of hope lay within,
touched with time and ageless strength!
Though leaves may wither,
beauty remains.

Throughout life's ages,
beauty sings her song.
She remains through the ages;
beauty always remains strong!

Silent Question

When was the last time your lips were kissed
with the passion you desired?
Yes, a desire only passion brings!
When was the last passionate fire?

When were you held so tight
and passionately kissed through the night?
How long have you been deprived;
how long have you survived?

Deprive not your lips no more,
for those lips I do adore.
I long to hold you tight,
both through the day and passionate night!

Deprive me not those lips, I pray,
nor to hold you close all life's way.
I want to love you through the night
with passion's song in our flight.

As your heart beats close to mine,
our passionate desires together entwine!

The Truth of God's Love

Beauty comes in many ways,
yet true beauty is from within.
Redeemed by love, God's healing power,
we live in hope and His grace each hour.

Knowing the truth of God's love,
I see true beauty from above!
Should I look another way?
No! For pure love I see every day.

One

One loves for what they can get,
the other loves for what they have.

One loves for what they can be,
the other loves for what they see.

One lives to please themselves,
the other lives to love.

When one gets all they can see
that pleases them, then what will be?

The other always has love
and loves what they see—
lives love and forever free!

One loves a loveless life,
while the other loves today this life!

Truth for the Day

Love of one's faded dreams and a passion of desire,
hidden in the heart of love's warm internal fire.
I feel love's passionate flames,
yet your love I can't acquire.
From within I still hold you close
with my heart's pounding attire.

Yet in respect I live distantly close by your side.
With truth from within, without I do hide.
For love's words do not fade amidst truth's tides;
amidst the sea of life's short-lived ride.

As I wait to see a glimpse of you,
an hour, a moment, oh heart so true!
Yet life abides and wades into
the beauty you bring, amidst the sky of blue.

My Loving You

You are my friend and the one I love;
you reach deep into the inner chamber of my heart.
A place of honor I set for you;
none other there sits, none but you.

Loved for life in this forever space,
a place enthroned by each heartbeat's place.
Every breath I take from end to start,
I love you, friend, from within my heart!

I long to sit close by your side;
tell you truths, I will not hide.
From morning to evening and all through the night,
I desire to listen to you and your beauty's sight!

Life's Situational Space

I sit and hold you in my arms, even while apart.
I kiss your lips, while in a separate place,
yet loving in my heart,
separated by life's situational space.

I hold you close!
You are not near,
yet I am close.
I hold you dear.

Separated, yet together,
as I hold you close.
Forever in love's truth,
there you I find!

Rehearsal

If life was able to be rehearsed
and re-worked, line by line,
I would write your name in each verse
and speak it sweet and kind!

Each verse re-lived in love you'd find.

Pure beauty speaks each movement
this story would give love, would live.
Each verse, each word, each solitary line—
perfection in life's beautiful sway.

For it would speak of you both night and day!

The Man

I sit in the corner aware of who I am—
the man I have become!
Aware of all my fears and desires;
aware of my own life's failures.

Who am I? I long to answer.
Yet I have no answers,
no idea of who I am!
Only the life I have lived and do live.

Not so lucky in love, this I bear as a pain.
Not so content within me, this is what I hold as a truth.
I am a heart who cares for those who accept me as I am—
it's my desire to be accepted by all I meet.

Time reminds me not all are so kind,
but a loving man I choose to be!
One who can live with all imperfections,
losses, pains, sorrow, and shame.

Yet refuses to lose the me that I am,
to those who choose to live a bitter, angry stand.
Hate I will not nor live their pain,
for all in the end, this man's truth remains.

Words

Words run around my head,
circles around my mind,
and lead my pen in hand,
revealing what I find
as word by word circles unwind.

A word picture of painted dreams;
a fictitious world's written schemes!
A poet's mind revealed to you,
from a pen to a hand, words to you.
From this a foreign land of rhythm and rhyme.

Placed in sweet beating time,
as you see this majestic flow,
with pen in hand, watch it grow.
All along the steps I take,
as a song, a poem, today I make!

Truly True

Walls and halls and window sills,
running around in my mind.
Calls and stalls within myself,
as mindfully I stumble blind.

Without there stands a stunning still,
I search within my soul!
To see the me I already knew,
and face the me that's true!

For all is within the Master's hand,
and of truth by grace I stand.
Not myself or who I am,
but truth by grace I am!

A Beautiful Mess

Mankind, a beautiful mess—
God's perfect creation!
His love, our salvation.

Created for His pleasure,
our love He does treasure.

Yet due to stubborn desires,
we live in striving acquires!

So what makes our anger breed,
as we ourselves daily bleed?

Unless we seize the day in a worshipful way,
as we live our best in our dysfunctional mess.

With hope within for a place to begin,
knowing only God's grace,
can keep us warmly in place!

Day Comes

The day comes
as light shines!
Hours and minutes,
day turns to night.

A day comes
as we live,
for this day
and God's praise.

The light's ray
along the way,
as we pray
a day comes.

Like no other,
as we live
this perfect day!

Yvonne

A pretty smile,
a gentle way,
a soft word—
what a day!

You bring light
within one's sight.
Kind-hearted girl,
God's created pearl.

Your smile,
your way,
soft words—
it's all ok!

Acceptance

Do you know what others see,
when you ask, what of me?
Will they like what will be?
What will they speak, speak of me?

Do you long to know what of me?
Or simply say what will be will be!
Others are not who is me,
for of myself to me I'm free!

Others well may put me down,
yet to myself I'll wear no frown.
For in what others think, I do not drown!

Pleasure

Whispering wind, you gently blow,
and across my face I feel you flow.
Nature's joy, a simple pleasure,
brings me peace beyond measure.

Wind, you greet me
with all your treasure.
Oh sweetly I feel
life's pleasure.

Gently, we greet
and now entwine.
Partaking in a dance,
both yours and mine!

Gleefully grand, fully in a trance,
together we two do now romance.
As nature's course, my heartfelt stance,
together we two live in life's dance.

How Sweet

Sweet is the day I see Your face,
and feel the warmth of Your embrace!
For only love, Your loving grace,
can joyfully fill my empty space.

Sweet the day, I learned to pray!
Sweet the day, all burdens I lay!
At Your feet, oh so sweet,
my Lord, so sweet that glorious day!

When before Your feet, I learned to pray!

Truly Me

On a mountain somewhere away from where I am,
dreaming about where I have been.
Looking for answers to where I was before,
knocking and beating on my own front door!

It's all right; it's ok,
dreaming about tomorrow, me getting in my way.
Making amends to myself never crossed my mind;
to myself it's ok to walk around blind.

It's all right; I'm ok,
lying to myself throughout the day.
When will I see beyond selfish me?
For it's truth to myself that makes me truly free!

Room

Beauty illuminates in the room's natural light,
as it reflects across her lips and skin so fair.
Brown golden hair flows down her neck's delight,
as eyes of blue gaze forward in flight.

Sensuous light rolls down her body,
revealing what God beautifully and perfectly created.
God's creative wonder, man's sheer delight,
lying there in nature's pure light.

Does she know her beauty's sight?
A complex wonder of heaven's delight.
Taking my very breath away,
as I sit, entranced in her sight!

Healing

Man calms his sleepless soul,
in peace he lies, no motion!
But a breath, motionless,
yet life within calms his soul.

Calms the day!
Calms this hour!
This moment in time,
deep within man's busy soul.

Calmness and peace stills the waves,
finally resting on this peaceful hour.
Calming his restless soul,
for this now is his healing hour!

God Defeats

Not quite but almost there;
on my way, who can compare?
Live and breathe, not always fair;
free to myself with nothing to compare.

On my way, not sure where,
but I'm on my way—I'll meet you there!
On my way without a care;
yes, on my way, no burdens to bear.

For on my way He guides my feet;
on my way He gives me food to eat!
On my way there is no defeat;
on my way with my Lord, so sweet!

On my way through life's testing heat;
on my way this world to beat.
On my way in victory I greet.

On my way, never alone,
for God defeats from His throne!

You Fight

Are you alone,
or do you live in a box?
Do you groan
when you say goodbye?

Is it just a waiting game,
as we live from day to day?
Each moment seems just the same,
or is it a lie we sing over again?

If you're choosing to live a lie,
as you look to see just why,
step out of the shell you live in!

Reach out your hand!
It won't bite, nor pull you in.
Like lies and her sinking sands,
give it up—it won't let you down!

Yet waiting on the other side,
you need not fear, just hold on tight!
Enjoy the truth!
No more do fight!

Encourager of My Heart

Encourager of my heart, this night,
thank you for coming to me,
for with your words you console my soul!

Blurred by emotions, I fight;
you made me to see right.
To you I will always be
a child in his daily flight.

Yet though I tend to lose my sight,
you are always gracious and the comfort of my soul;
my song of peace on a stormy day,
and warmth of hope to light my way!

The Hand

From the writer's heart
comes a melody of words.
Some in rhythm, some in time,
tied together in rhythm and rhyme!

Is this a talent to do,
or simply a part of what he knew?
The only answer is beyond;
the pen and paper in which he is fond!

How does he? What does he?
It's not simply what you see,
but a gift of God
that guides his hand.

And the hand of God
is the final plan.

My Last Goodbye

Wandering through a winter's storm,
covering my head from the rain,
looking for a place to hide from.

In the hour of my deepest dream,
a place I long my life to be,
here I see a momentous desire,
a love of one's hope's fire.

A fulfilling place I long to acquire,
where I fulfill my own life-filled dreams,
moving beyond this world's schemes,
this place I capture within my heart.

In belated dreams 'tis my start,
fulfilling glimpses of this life's fire,
which leads my life no more to tire,
but leads me on to a lifelong song.

To this world I sing my last goodbye,
to live, to love, to know beyond.

Sharing Life's Bitter Pleasures

Amidst life's bitter treasures
lies a heart of past pain.
Past is all that does remain,
as I step into the present day.

Life-filled remain, 'tis life I do sustain,
as hour by hour my life now flowers.
A bright lively day, a purer life's way,
yet past is the ground around.

The faded past of life's refuge,
which feeds the seed of the me I am now.
It brings me hope and teaches me how—
how to live another day, how to keep the way.

Which makes me strong
and from truth not to stray.
For in life there are many bitter pleasures
that meet the day.

Yet in all this is a truth—
God leads me on to face each day.
Each hour, each moment,
along life's path and graceful day.

'Tis Spring

'Tis spring! Hurray!
The birds sing gay;
the sun shines bright
in a spring-filled delight.
For nature comes to light!

Spring now sings,
winter moves her way;
yes, 'tis now spring.
'Tis spring this day!

Sunshine fills the room
in a glorious way—
'tis spring, 'tis spring! Hurray!

If You Believe

If you believe,
you can receive
what you need,
beyond selfish greed.

Humbled in life,
stumbled in strife,
life can begin
beyond one's sin.

Does life begin
because it's fulfilled within?
If you believe!
If you deceive!

To self-grieve,
forget to believe,
look for choice
that gives you voice.

Clinging to life,
living in strife,
fear to begin,
lost in sin.

Believe, don't deceive;

receive, don't grieve;
laugh, don't cry;
trust, don't lie.

Be, don't flee;
Humble, don't stumble.
Use the right choice,
don't lose your voice.

Win, don't sin;
begin from within!

Pages and Pages

Pages and pages
of words, mine,
come all together
within my mind.

Ages and ages,
a word-full life,
flow as streams
from my mind.

Shining they gleam
in word-full flow,
one to two
together they grow.

A flowing bliss
of rhythmic flow,
word by word
beating in time.

Word upon word,
line upon line,
painting a picture
from my mind.

Fear

Why do I sit in a cloudy gray,
while tears within me stray?
Now fear I the way I see;
sadly, 'tis of my own decree.

Alas this my own heavy heart;
it weighs me down where I start.
So why do I sit in my own dismay,
as before me sits a glorious day?

Fearing the me I fear I see,
yet truth before my eyes breathes.
I sit in tensed by internal lies,
fearing what will be of my own demise!

Oh fear I now the man I am,
in search for truth's hidden plan.
As there before my mortal cries,
my God, He sees my hurtful sighs.

He warms my aching soul,
brings me peace, and makes me whole.

The Day

Lies live in the day I choose,
and distrust I all but booze!
In a drunken stupor's bottle's sip,
deeper and deeper without a grip.

Drunkenness of my own mind
leads me to my own kind.
Lost in desires, I forget to begin,
till a sober moment leaves me spin.

Grabbing the hope, I think I cope,
and fearing within I fear to begin.
So drunk and numb,
I choose to be dumb.

Lies live in the day I choose;
tell me what do I lose?

Clouds

In a grateful mind, peace I find,
floating all around my mind.
A soft gentle loving heart
allows a place to restart.

As clouds softly hover in the sky,
I see my truthful place in sight.
Yet fear I not the day to come,
nor feel my world's life undone.

Clouds delight my every day,
though storms may cause a hint of gray.
I live on within this sway,
as I live to hope, come what may.

Loving a Woman

Soft and gentle though beauty may be,
I thank my God I am free.
Not that I despise the beauty in my eyes,
but fear the me in what I see.

This fragile beauty I do see,
a strong loving woman, can she really love me?
Or can I love her as I choose?
Confused I am in my own shoes!

Soft and gentle a woman may be;
God keep me strong on my own to be free!

Sure

A chill crosses my face,
a gust of fall's air.
What a morning's joy,
the wind across my face!

As I see this world's cares,
I know hope is there.
God's gentle hand,
majestically planned!

Through these simple eyes,
truth beyond lies.
My life feels simple peace;
a peace that only God can release.

As days and years are here and gone,
what can one see, but truth!
Or live a lie till truth is all that remains;
the chill of a life lost, beaten and dead in life's frost!

Teasing Rain

The teasing rain goes from slow to hard,
falling on the window pane,
reminding me of who I am,
Rain falling, hear her sound,
it disappears into the ground.

As life and her journey end,
we fall from birth to mold,
for time stands still for none we know.
Yet in life flowers grow,
and need the falling rain so.

Water the seeds in life we know,
as tomorrow comes never late.
We all help life's seeds,
whether small or great.

Crow's Nest

High above the mast and sail,
above the waves in the wind and hail,
I sit and ponder night to day,
to warn of danger's disarray!
Oh wind, blow not your cold decay,
but sun and moon shine!

Sea calm, please smoothly sail;
keep my wits that I not fail!
Let us glide across your water's flow,
oh mercy be, the God I know!
Keep me warm as a woolen glove;
direct me, please, the God I love!

As I sit high, up in the sky,
grant me peace, direct my eyes!
Let me not sleep in the night;
grant me strength to see just right!
This lonely place, grant me sight,
that I may see a peaceful flight!

I Long for the Walls

I long for the walls around me,
to hold peace within.
For the ceiling above me,
to shelter me from above.

I long for a place,
a home free from the outside malaise.
A quiet place to call alone;
a sweet display of peace.

Ah, I dream of a home;
a warm spot all mine!
I dream, but alas I have not;
I long for walls around.

The walls I have are cold,
weather-worn by the years.
A leaky roof that lets in rain;
I know no peace, yes none is known.

Yet I will not cease, till I'm home!

Today

Thunder rolls across my eyes,
as blue-gray sky, a wind wept sky,
ignites the desert wind's reply,
while palm trees dance melodiously high.

A light rain peppers the sand;
I stand in awe of God's command.
Freshly my lungs do inhale,
for of myself I am but frail.

Complexly simple, God created day;
Simply complex in my own minute way.
I live and breathe by His graceful hand,
and by His peace this is where I stand.

Across My Mind

A thousand words across my mind
could not describe one so kind.
A million miles across the day
could not bring a heartless sway.

For if I see and hear no more,
I know You're there at my door.
A trillion dreams of fame I might
look to You to make it right.

All I see and know so well,
You have me here within Your spell.
A billion dreams and sleepless nights,
I see Your smile, and You make it right!

So where do I go, but in Your sight,
for God I know You help me fight.
And win I will for upon that hill,
that bloodstained ground, I was found!

A thousand words across my mind
could not describe love so kind!

Tireless is Life

As the hourglass of each day,
we live moment by moment.
Through skies of blue's bitter gray,
time moves on till 'tis no more to be!
Each day living a hope of another moment to see.

Yet alas, moments slow to a place's end,
yet of truth, tireless we tire less.
To one day no more to see,
and all we fear to be 'tis no more in this life,
as we move on free!

Whiskey Bottle

Innocence fears the momentary profound.
I see nothing in the end of the day;
I hear only a bit of gray.
I sing but what lyrics? What tune?

As I stare into the glass,
I see only a forgotten mime;
forgotten by the intoxicating flow.
The forgotten time's roll!

A buzz, a polluted moment,
numbs to the world I fear.
To many profoundly complex ways,
as I strive for peace of days!
A whiskey bottle numbing my fear.

Life is what life sees,
through the whiskey bottles.
Life now becomes clearly hazy,
in the crazy sense of drunken gear.

I sit, I drink, and from life steer,
callously numb drunk from the life I own.
A buzz, a polluted moment;
a great escape from what I fear!

Rising Sun

The morning song helps me arise,
from life's fears in which I sleep.
From the ruins of fears to fears,
I arise to stand on my feet.

From my crippling despair,
and from my knees, I take God's hand.
There He lifts me from my knees
and in love heals my broken heart!

He dries my bed of tears,
as the nothing in me breathes.
Life comes to a wounded heart,
as I see my reflection in the broken glass.

Expose the wrinkles of aged time
and beyond the flower of youth life fades.
My heart knows the youthfulness of my skies
and on the other side, I see the me I've known.

Once cold as a lifeless stone,
yet now arisen from my lies.
To see above God's majestic skies
and the rising of the Son to live again.
Knowing truth is found in God's healing hand.

Life's Rebel Songs

The ayre of life's rebel songs,
fill the mountains bright,
as the breeze of change floats on by.
Tomorrow sees another way,
and the faded songs turn to gray.

A once desirous cause is lost in time,
now to become a historic chime,
of hurtful wars and bitter hearts,
of fatherless children and widows' cries.

A musty book of historic times,
a dusty look at what once was,
and what now we see or thought to be,
as this ayre fills the mountains high!

We look, we hope, we sing along,
till what we believe moves on,
and in time sings on life's ayre,
man's rebel songs.

Christine

Why do I find the years so kind,
and you still heavy on my mind?
A smile of gold, a warm heart's glimmer,
as the pain of truth still causes me to shiver.

For my heart does speak your gentle name,
yet I fear in life, my dear.
No more a cheer, for my heart love is clear;
love's refrain, for to you love still remains.

Yet gentle heart, I pray, that your love may hold me,
somewhere in your memory, kind,
and alas one day to find,
a piece of this heart you left behind.

The Four Corners

The four corners sing aloud a dance,
for all who come and wish to glance.
A fiddler, a tenor, a pipe or two,
traditions dance before the eyes for you.

Welcome all to join right in;
don't ask for a place, just come begin.
These corners know a joy or two,
and welcome all, not just a few!

Come see, 'tis all for free.
Beyond the gray or bright blue sky,
come and dance, just come on by!

The Way

Truth comes as a flaming fire,
bringing peace to one's desire,
quenching this life's deceitful mire.
In His peace you know, for God's truth is no liar!

Truth calms across the day,
calming with honest display,
beyond the fear of life's black to gray.
Truth brings pure truth to the way!

Listening to Dylan

Standing with hands out,
sitting with head down,
lying out in the night,
walking by while looking beyond.

The day turns to night,
is there something wrong?
While the chosen true,
turn blind eyes to the needful view.

Is this what makes us strong?
As music of the passing day turns to a lament;
is there something wrong?
The lyrics of honesty's song.

Recite a tear or two by passing honest true,
turning to see sufferings decree.
Any doubt in the painful about?
There is something wrong.

Out of key we sing honesty's song!
Can we sing along? Can we sing while we mourn?
In the day, as truth comes our way,
is there something wrong?
Or has ignorance rewritten this song?

What For?

A man lies dead on the street somewhere;
a child cries in hunger, in fear!
A woman lies battered and bruised;
man is elected to the life he does choose!

A heart pounds for one final time;
a baby born to a life, not so kind!
Why fear another tear when inside we live—
hope we give!

Or lose as in the day we choose,
circled by a heart we learn the truth.
We see the truth each and every day,
a hopeful way in this world's crushing pain.

Fear we the day,
yet in God's hands,
we fear beyond the day!
In hope we see a better way.

For the hope and love of life,
and hope in the common we stand.
As God holds us, dazed and confused,
firmly in His loving hands.

Dundalk

I walk through times and memories of my youth—

The sooty streets and fireplaces bright,
meet the air of the misty night!
Streets and homes of years past flight.

I see my brother, who is now gone,
the two of us playing on the front yard lawn.
A tear, a smile, I sit awhile,
till the sun's warmth is gone.

A smile to part, time to move on,
as I embrace the moment
with my brother, Sean.

This town of the past,
yet so differently the same.
Cracks and tracks of the paths I knew.

The sidewalks sing a reminiscent tune—

Step upon step, imbedded in my mind;
smiling, I inhale my past pleasantness, so kind.
Dundalk, my youth, in newness past unfolds!

The town square, Oriel Park, my memories freshly old;

my feet lead me on,
as the past takes me home.

Steps of memories, time so real and not forgotten;
walking the streets as my memories define.
Loving joy sprinkled with a little pain in time.

My life, these streets, together time meets.
The town!
Now home to a time I have known!

Acknowledgements

I wish to thank my daughter, Kraetsel, and son, Michael, for their love and support; and my big sister, Mary McLoughlin (Mary Mc), who has always displayed unconditional love and total support through my life!

Pastor Erik Sahakian, who always has a kind word and has supported me in times of struggle—you are a Godsend to me!

I also wish to dedicate this book to the memory of my dad, Thomas O'Connor (1922-1989), the greatest dad ever; and my little brother, Sean (1963-2007). I miss you Seanie-boy and I know now you and Dad are dancing in heaven.

About the Author

Michael G. O'Connor is retired from a 30-year career in mental health. He regularly travels to Ireland, serves in the local community, and writes. Mike has a deep passion to show people that peace is not a destination; instead, peace is a journey. His love for his Savior is the foundation for the hope he shares in his work.